UNCONVENTIONAL

BY
CLARA BENICE

UNCONVENTIONAL

ISBN 978-0-6151-8531-6

Address comments to:
email: unconventional7@gmail.com

Edited by Rebecca Barnes
Cover Photo by Clara Benice

Dedicated to you for not conforming to conventions...

QUESTIONS?

What is it all about?
Does anyone really know?
Why do I want to know what it is about?
Is there an answer?
Who has the answer?
Why am I writing about this question?
Why ask what is it all about?
What is about?
What is all?
What is it?
What is is?
What is what?
What is??
What
Is
?

I AM...

Free to laugh
Free to cry
Free to dance
Free to eat
Free to sleep
Free to speak
Free to love
Free to be

FEELINGS AND MORE

I didn't want to feel again
Each time I felt it reminded me of you.
It felt like there was no truth to our moments.
I believed it and stopped feeling.
Then I realized that each moment was truthful
We were true to the present but not the future.
Knowing that made me feel again.

ONE STEP

Nice seeing you the other day...
You said to me.
I can't answer
It would mean so much more to me.
It was nice to hear, but you could've kept it
It's the implication not the meaning
So, please don't try to be nice
It won't help me get over you.

MUAH!

Two moons ago...
Your warm lips caressed
My cheeks, neck and more...
Kissing you has been a great experience
One sometimes I wish to replicate
But after the kisses all is lost.

LOSS

The pain is so deep
Each time I take a breath
It reminds me of the loss
Each time I release a breath
It reminds me of what was.

LULLABY

Doom doom! Doom doom!
Doom doom! Doom doom!
That's what your heart sings
Doom doom! Doom doom!
Reminder that you are here
Doom doom! Doom doom!
Don't take away this moment
Doom doom! Doom doom!
Shhh! Listen to the song
Doom doom! Doom doom!
Your heart is calling me

ANSWERS!

We all seek answers
We all give answers
We all store answers
We all want answers
We all need answers
We all love answers
We all deserve answers

LATE CALL

Ring... Ring...
Hey...
How are you?
Fine...
What are you doing?
Sitting...
You?
Watching TV
Good for you
Well... can you come over
Over?
My house...
Need to feel your warmth...
Sorry...
Goodnight!
Goodnight...

LOVE LIKE...

I love you like a child hungry for her mother's milk
Like the sunlight on the moon at night
Like hearing your favorite song on the radio
Like morning dew on a newly blossomed flower
Like an old couple on a park bench making out
Like a puppy playing with her favorite toy
Like an intense orgasmic sensation
Like pralines and cream Haagen Daz ice cream
Like no other love before
I love you simply because I do.

MIDSUMMER NIGHT

As the moon sets and gets ready to rest,
You knock, and I let you in with a welcoming smile.
Inside... my house is alive again
You wake up the sleeping beauty
And find a warm place to settle
Creating a perfect fit.
As the waters flow, we travel deep into the summer night.

PETALS

Rough Engaging Mysterious Torment Recent Action
=
I Miss You But I Know I Should Stop Missing You

FIRST TIME

On the path of truth
Only righteous ones can prevail
Sorrow and pain will never
Replace the joy I felt
The first time we met

FALLING

Truth be told
I've fallen for you
Truth be told
I wish I did not fall for you
Truth be told
I'm not strong to stop falling for you
Truth be told
I don't want to stop falling
Truth be told
I should stop falling
Truth be told
I feel when I fall.

LIFE FORCE

Your life force
Takes me by surprise
Closes my eyes
And breathes you in
Releases the warmth
As it glides between my lips
Savors the joy of life
And holds me
Captive for one moment.

Mommy...
I miss you...
There's so much to say...
I believe you know it all...
Your daughter...

TOUCH

Reach and touch
Just one touch
Up to touch
Wish you touch
Please do touch
Will you touch
Meet and touch.

SAY IT

Why call to casually say "Hi"?
If you don't say what you want.
It's confusing!
Just articulate your wants
Or let's move apart quietly.
Maybe this is the process to the end...

SAME FACE

Yesterday I saw your face
All became very clear
You're not the person
I fell in love with.
I don't like the new face,
But it is who you are
Wish I had known the truth then.

WIND DANCE

As the wind
Blows the leaves to dance, twirl and move to the next place
Something starts very low on the ground
To an explosion of joy high up in the air
Then slowly back down to the ground
But in a new place
Never back to the same place
Always moving to somewhere new blown by the wind
Only words can make sense of what this is
Yet even words cannot express it to anyone
But still in words we believe

VULNERABLE
My heart is as open as the sky
In any case life is always right

IT'S NOT PERSONAL

You broke me into pieces
Something I believed couldn't happen to me.
Not only did you break my heart
You kept on coming back to the crime scene
To break the pieces some more as if the first time was not
enough.
I don't know how to describe the pain I feel
You claim it's not personal
But I believe it is
Because of the excruciating pain I feel this instant.

PAIN

It hurts so much
I can't even cry out loud
I want to scream
But no sound is coming out
I want to run but I can't feel my legs
The only thing I can do
Is stand still.

WISHING NOT

I wish this could be pain free
I wish I'd protected my heart from you
I wish I didn't live life when we were together
I wish I'd lied to you
I wish I didn't wish that we never met

POST BREAKUP AD

I'm not angry
I'm just hurting

Wanted: A delete button to forget you

Pain + Pain = Death

Memories of you are swords piercing through my heart

I just want to cry. Tears of pain. Tears you don't see.

There's no painkiller for loving you

It's not personal but I am a person

Love is a luxury all of us can afford

YOU...

A sneak peek of
What's to come
A twinkle in your eyes
A crook in your smile
As you introduce yourself to me.

CIRCLE

The world is not...
Permanent
Enduring
Logical
It is full of...
Humaneness

NEW DAY

Today is a new day
New memories to be made
Another sunrise to welcome
Sweet smell of rain
On a Late Summer day
Melodious laughter of
Children playing.

JOY OF LIFE

Your heart beats loud enough for me to hear
With my hand on your chest feeling the rhythm of your life
Each beat reminds me that you are real and alive
So, I rest my hand to feel your warmth
As I listen to the beat of your heart.

PLAYTIME

Another day of fun and play
This time you are strong and confident
Each time you enter
I smile to welcome you
My body responds to your touch
But my heart hides until
We pass the day of fun

MOMENTS

What is it that makes life stop when we're together?
The moment I saw you
I knew the answer
Every second is a moment of intention
Life is ever changing
Each moment brings something new

ONLY ONE YOU...

One look
One smile
One touch
One scent
One kiss
One you

SILENCE

SILENCE IS...
sacred
SILENCE
important
SILENCE
what we want
SILENCE
the answer
SILENCE
the question
SILENCE
manifesto
SILENCE
obsolete
SILENCE
truth
SILENCE
beauty
SILENCE
eternal
SILENCE
worth more than words

SLEEPLESS MIND

All alone, back and forth
I want to know if you'll remember.
Is there room for me in the crowded room?
Yet on hold for when you need.
The inn is always open but
The innkeeper is never there
I sleep only to dream of the last moment.

LOSS OF CHILDHOOD

Searching for the child who ran for hours
Laughed for days without a need of something funny
When did she disappear?
Loud laughter
Racy footsteps
Free to be

DREAM WITH ME

Close your eyes
Dream with me for a moment
Let's journey together
Trust your heart with me
Let me lead you
One by one, step by step
Don't think
Just let yourself go
It's only us
Tonight you can be part of me
Tomorrow you'll wake up with a new dream

WHAT IF...

What if I write it all down?
There's not enough ink in my pen
What if I write it all down?
It will not mean as much to me anymore
What if I write it all down?
It will not save me from you
What if I don't write it all down?
Then what if...

RENDEZVOUS

Midnight rendezvous
Sweet smell of roses with rain
Walking hand in hand
Within our own pace
One jolt of laughter here and there
Endless gazing at each other
Moonlit path with unknown
Scary Sound yet harmless
Soft touch of skins
Gliding through the spaces
Only we can imagine

BEST OF TIMES

In the deep night
All the stars fall
Only for us to see
Standing near the fire
The only witnesses of this moment

BE STILL

It's hard to remain still and not do anything
But I'm learning to let go quietly
Why argue my case
When there is no jury to decide
Only one chance at life
Now I will sit quiet and wait.

BIRTH

From a silent place to an open fire full of violent flames
Life springs underneath it all
Assuming all properties
Though some never ignite
But it's the becoming of all
For we contribute to its forces
As it rains once more

LOVE SONG FOR DAFUR

I see your pain from the pictures
I hear your stories from the human right workers
I feel your despair and hopelessness from the documentaries
But yet I cannot reach you
I cannot stop you from getting killed, raped and tortured
I can't bring your family back to you
I can't give your home back
All I can do is stand with you
And sing a love song for you
Soon you'll stop hurting, dying and crying
So sing a love song for Dafur
Save Dafur
Save a woman
Save a man
Save a child

DREAM ON...

Dream on Dreamer
For only when you dream
Can your story come to life.
Stand for what you believe.
Go for what you want.
Work for where you need to go.
Smile for what you'll achieve.
Don't stop dreaming
Until you reach the top.
Dream but don't sleep.

UNCONVENTIONAL LOVE

Feel your spirit
Examine your breath
Take in all that life has to offer
Look at the sunrise
Smell the flowers
Shower in the sunrays
Sleep under the moonlight
Sing with the leaves
Fly with the birds
Dance with the wind
Rest with the lake
Flow with the river

CREATION

Each moment
Each time
While you're here
Make the best of it

Each day
Each night
As you rest
Make life's nest

NEW BEGINNINGS

What's next?
One step at a time
Leading to
A path of joy
A future of hope
Songs and dances
Nightfall for dreams
Moonset awakes the sun.

EACH MOMENT COUNTS

Seasons change
Life changes
People change
Time passes
Uncertainties remain
And Love prevails.

Tomorrow is today
A memory of yesterday
You either have it or not
No regrets...Thank God that
Behind are memories and pictures
Each moment counts.

Circle A and B

All I want to do is transformed to this other being. I don't remember at what point she arrived and I stepped aside. I became her and even say that I am she. Her breath is mine, her looks are mine, and her voice is mine. I recognize her because she is I. She took control and gained what she wanted. She did not give it much thought like I would have.

She closes her eyes and behaves as if no one else exists even the one who made this experience possible. The transformation is quick and unrecognizable. With a release in the atmosphere confirmed by the warmth and the wetness of her body. As the end of the transformation approaches it becomes clear for me to return and for her to wait in the distance until next time.

BEWARE

I say that I would not open the gates again. But I saw you from my balcony and something traveled in the space to connect us. Yet I was not going to let you in. Not on my grounds. But somehow talking through the gates became a dangerous game. Before I could gather my next thought you were in my living area having tea. I struggled with the thoughts of you inside my house. But I was not strong to fight you maybe I did not want to fight anymore. So, I signed the entry papers to let you through the gates and inside my home at your convenience. Immediately you were in my bedroom. I woke up one day and you were here staring and telling me how much you appreciate me. And how I make you insane. You called yourself addicted to me. But I can't have tea or take care of you because I found out that you are a thief and your next project is to steal my goods. So I'm determined to keep you out and away.

WISH

Some wish for rain
Some wish for sun
Some wish for money
Some wish for youth
Some wish for health
Some wish for beauty
Some wish for intelligence
Some wish for common sense
Some wish for rest
Some wish for food
Some wish for happiness
Some wish for good times
All wish for love
One wish for you
I wish for a moment

IF ONLY...

If only... we were not afraid of sharing what we feel inside.
If only... you told me your fears
If only... I told you that I hadn't laughed or cried so hard until I met you.
If only... you would stop trying to figure out what you think I want
If only... you would enjoy our stolen moments together
If only... I did not hear your heart beat
If only... our paths never crossed
If only... you did not steal the key to my heart
If only... I did not look into your eyes and soul
If only... I could stop my heart from the pain
If only... I knew what tomorrow will bring
If only... you could answer all my questions
If only... I could stop loving you
If only... we could meet again
If only... If only... If only....

Manny...
Funny how my heart still aches like it was yesterday.
Sometimes I wish that it was a bad nightmare.
Yet, I find tremendous strength to go on.
Eureka!

HONESTLY...

If I tell you how much I love you...
You say you don't deserve my love...
For now my heart is with you...

HIM...

As each night falls she dreams of him. But in the day she erases him from her mind to proceed with the details of her day.

What does she want from him? She can't truly answer that question. She has a few ideas but she is not quite sure if she has the true answer.

He doesn't know what to do with her because she is not like anyone he knows or had relations with. But her spirit and essence are intoxicating. He keeps on coming back for more. He throbs at the sound of her voice. Her piercing almond shaped eyes are hypnotic vehicles to his lost soul. He is able to see himself when looking at her. Her sexuality drives him insane and asking for more. Her brilliant mind is poisonous to his thoughts when they communicate in harmony.

He is the Adam to her Eve, the milk to her café au lait, and the umbilical cord to her baby.

NATURAL CAUSES

Dancing leaves
Diamond shaped
Yellow trees
What will become of you?

Dark cloud
Rough wind
Falling Rain
Where will you hide?

Sun Showers
Clear Sky
Blossoming Tulips
Who will remain true?

IN LOVE WITH LOVE

This is what it is
I don't know how to explain it
All I know is that I like you more than I can express.
I'm not sure when it happened.
I like the idea of my heart and mind working together to care
for you.
I am taking a big step by even writing this down
But I know what I want and I am willing to stand and support
it.
You are the one that I want and I choose you.
My heart smiles at the sound of your voice
You tell me that I have some type of power
Maybe... but it's all because of the way I feel about you.

MOVEMENTS

The leaves are falling
Snow is coming
The benches are empty
Sounds of the wind whisper in the distance
Piano keys speaking to my soul
Keys playing softly saying to listen and dance
Movements of the moment guide the keys
Up and down
Right and left
Open and close
Lift and drop

LOTS OF WORDS

Garden of roses all colors of the sunrays
Happy are the petals for life shines on them to show off their
beauty. The smell of roses is intoxicating it calms the body
yet excites its senses to open the windows to the chambers
that are closed. How lucky are the rose petals to be loved by
the wind and the sun. One caresses them the other takes them
on a journey.
Where the petals are part of the flowers or the ground.

LET GO

Let it go anywhere it wants to go,
Wherever it wants to go.
Go away, far away, go somewhere
Go anywhere go I don't know where
Wherever it goes – let go leave.
Take me with you, why I don't know
I don't want to go
I don't know why I'm writing because you must let go.
Let go of what?
Just LET GO!

YELLOW ROSE

The yellow rose is not as pretty as the red rose
Not As sensual as the pink rose
Not As classic as the white rose

It brings peace without overwhelming presence as calmness
and serenity follow her.

Take a long look and remain in its presence
You'll see sunshine, happiness, security, loyalty,
Hope, optimism, timidity and above all beauty.

Its innocence brings unconditional love.

To SM

The art of writing flowers consciousness and truth.
Anything can be used to find truth.
Use your pen and write to unlock the mysteries of existence,
word after word.
Each word is a door opening to you.
The doors will continue to open because there's no end to this
journey.
So find yourself in your own words.

SPIRITUAL ESSENCE

Haunted by the essence of a sweet spirit
I yearn to see what wraps around my being
One can only tell what one feels
I smell and feel your presence
Feelings of loss but not of hopelessness
If only I could touch or see you
Seeking for something lost that can never come back or be
found

...

www.ingramcontent.com/pod-product-compliance
Lightning Source LLC
LaVergne TN
LVHW091209080426
835509LV00006B/904